Well Waiting Room

POETS OUT LOUD

Elisabeth Frost, *series editor*

Well Waiting Room

Stephanie Ellis Schlaifer

Fordham University Press   New York   2021

Fordham University Press has no responsibility for the
persistence or accuracy of URLs for external or third-party
Internet websites referred to in this publication and does
not guarantee that any content on such websites is, or will
remain, accurate or appropriate.

Fordham University Press also publishes its books in a
variety of electronic formats. Some content that appears in
print may not be available in electronic books.

Visit us online at www.fordhampress.com.

Library of Congress Cataloging-in-Publication Data

Names: Schlaifer, Stephanie Ellis, author.
Title: Well waiting room / Stephanie Ellis Schlaifer.
Description: First edition. | New York : Fordham University
    Press, 2021. | Series: Poets out loud
Identifiers: LCCN 2021016623 | ISBN 9780823297771 (trade
    paperback)
Subjects: LCGFT: Poetry.
Classification: LCC PS3619.C414 W45 2021 | DDC
    811/.6—dc23
LC record available at https://lccn.loc.gov/2021016623

Printed in the United States of America

22 21 20   5 4 3 2 1

First edition

For Arny

We're still waiting for the President to tweet.

—Yamiche Alcindor, *PBS NewsHour*, March 22, 2019

Contents

Well Waiting Room

The Ambassador of the Interior Has a Talking-to with the Minister of the Cabinet of Vengeance

God started small   At the first showdown
between good and evil   God didn't come at anyone

like a cowboy   God didn't open with solar flares
or asteroids   or mass extinction   or planetary heat death

God didn't outgun anyone   God outmanned them
God made man   in the face of the beast

And in the face of the beast God made   from inside
the great and gaping maw   while languishing

in the hot damp   in the face of that
great terror   God summoned the smallest—

adrenaline   serotonin   hemoglobin   oxytocin   motes
of possibility   God started by making—

light into landmasses   sand into vessels   preservation
as civilization   And sometimes   God won

A Member of the Cabinet of Culpabilities Challenges the Cabinet's Minister

We all wanted the same thing   but things ripped
open   pink flesh on
gold thrones   the bones of
empires   Golden avenues of sunset-

light   gold in every
helping   of rotting
flesh   that birds came to

feast upon   They called
and we
feasted   We feasted

on it   We pushed our beaks into
eyelids   into follicles   into
yolky membranes   We pecked things
down to the socket   and mellowed

at the yellowing edges   We memorized
what we'd cannibalized   (selectively
in pictures)   at the backs
of our eyes

while everything   looked like   smelled like   tasted like
butter   everything with an odor

of fat   The air inside us was thick
with riches   and we lapped
at it   We gnawed ourselves

from rib   to nipple
to bloody breast   until

we couldn't tell   one thing
from another

Dictation from the Autocrat of the Interior

Stephanie   dash   I'm writing because I want a new —
president — a different moment   — a different moment feels
like a different moment feels like — the future — Right now the
future is — dealing cacao — dealing with rivals — dealing with
— Starting again — Stephanie — dash — I'm writing you from —
the future — from — a hideout in the mountains — I'm having a
wonderful time — It's Pavlovian this time of year — Stop — I'm
here because I wonder — whether the current limbo can be toppled
— No — overcome — ? — Stephanie — question mark — I'm
hoping you can help me — Can you tell me whether you can help
me — build the infrastructure — of a different moment — where
— the weapon of choice isn't   — humanitarian aid — isn't —
humans — isn't — a war that's not a war — doesn't have   — a
non-disparagement clause — a smile — a nod — a thumb's up
— bracketed by — horrific tales of violence — But the future
Stephanie — The future is — 99% hyperinflation — 100% under
our noses — The state — The state of — right where we're sleeping
— the drugs still flowing — The children taking turns cooking
— The brutality — The brutal — new — light

Open Letter to the Minister of the Cabinet of Denial
(The Quick)

Antarctica is calving   and we are
broken below the whites   There's no

umbilicus that tethers us
to a less sordid past   The sun will always

take the mother with the young
Try and separate

your yolk from the threshold
of humanity   see what fissures

You, too, could heave
a dead but breathing thing

a monster of man and woman
borne   of brine and oxygen

a salty molecule   cleaved
quick and dangerous

Don't say you never saw it
coming   Don't say you have a hold

on what breaks free from you

The Cabinet of Slippery Slopes

The flow of the jet stream is the flow of information

At 35,000 feet the atmosphere becomes more predictable but less
    reliable

Talk to me about surer footings

I want the absolute truth

A figure is not a picture

In a high pressure system   everyone wears a mask

Gilding gives the illusion of worth   In a figure   this is the
    illusion of depth

Economies are illusions in pictorial space

Currencies are drawn on   and he was *such* a bad artist

People traveling in the same direction imply a system of belief

In this figure to ground relationship   you are going the wrong
    way

A mask is a kind of silence

In a picture   the shadow of a cloud impinging upon a mountain is
    a negotiation

In nature   it is a futility

A good illusion tells you exactly what you're looking for

I don't believe in the devil   I believe I can beat him

Arrows travel in the direction you expect of them

The cells are everywhere   Look at Cedar Rapids   Look at Iran

Look at each other

But the trajectory of your body   arrowphobic

A shadow enterprise can leave a huge portion of the map
    unaccounted for

Cover your bases

Cover your eyes

MEMORANDUM *(We have to do it all again)*

The clouds darkened
and the rains came
dragging old dirt
into a new year

—some pigment
a thawing January ochre

Metaphor
for the thing about to happen

Someone has to take the animal
Someone   turn the hair to brush
Someone has to make the paint   the painting
the animal on the cave wall

From the Cabinet of Counterweights & Measures

The raincloud floated swiftly by
   It floated   exuberantly
   lavishly, even   with admirable speed
   as though it were a barge
   (and urgently)
   with somewhere to go

And beneath its gouache-gray hull
you were   demonstrably marveling   at the living
patterns   of water   on water   on water

What is the weight of it worth to you?
   Its underbrushing
   Its sea of seas

       Is it captained? Navigable?

Can it steer the stations of your discord   wide and barren
as a moor?

For you are standing in a rising water—

the air is evident   the air, an exit   the air, untethered
barrage balloons

Why not reach upwards? Rush headlong?
It is magnificent!

For here is nothing:
a drowsy, creatureless rain
where you are an idler   some tiny thing
frantically waving its hands

The Documentarian of the Interior Opposes the Bill from the Minister of the Cabinet of Nostalgia

after Paul Cornoyer's "The Plaza after the Rain," after Saint Gaudens'
"William Tecumseh Sherman"

for Douglas Dowd

All monuments commemorate the same
falsehood   The gilt is genuine and we feel it right

at the surface of our discontent
Anger   like so many lustrous mounts   softens

in the rain   And stallions and generals must periodically be
re-gilded   recommitted to   as if

an abiding law of man
Though   if we are honest   it is the law that fails us

along with what we can abide   The fiction
that what prevailed was   thence purifying   thence pure

thenceforth glint and glistening—see how your face shines
in thy horse's arse!   See how the lie defines

a nation ever after   North & South   brother from brethren
boots from pavement   ideals from dirt

all heaven in the sky   which all falls
raining   if Cornoyer's brush is on the level   Just

cobble   and cornice   and hoofy mount   opaquely
bronzed behind us   Aforehand

sooty   puddled shadows   God   standing in the laws
we made   God   standing in the light

The Cabinet of Ontology

for Ron Leax

There were many ways of being in the world   The body made
a list
            Extemporaneously   Judiciously   Fruitlessly   Wantonly
Indecorously   Unabidingly   Imprudently   close to death

The body experienced everything
as a weather event   water in all the wrong places

The body thought of itself
as a diatomaceous thing   taxon to phylum
cut in two   The body asked

Are we not whole   if we are not wholly of
one mind?   We are not   but (yet) as

        salt
     and chrysophytum
     and polypeptides
     and algum
     and simple sugars
     and sticky things
     and chains of acids
     and volatile oils
     and hydrogenation
     and collagens
     and noble gases
     and osmotic membranes
     and things that store as starch

we are   (as so many things)   in unison

The body ferried itself out of the damp
It convened   and reconvened

From the Cabinet of Origin Stories

Yellow is spring's first eruption.
Spring, the Earth's,
Earth, the darkness's
and darkness, from the mouth of God.

The mouth of God erupts
as weeds.

As: *dandelion.*

Or: *buttercup.*

Perennially. Sometimes errantly,
late winter, and survives the ice.

Erumpent daffodils,
insistent with their trumpets,
bay the bright forsythia,
bear your longing forth.

The almost-reaching raceme
of the asphodel—
a corruption of the near-dark earth.

The earth warms at the mouth of God,
in this sequence of excrescence.
From slime mold on old leaves
to sweet rot into the air releasing.

At that sight or with this scent,
one pleasant afternoon becomes every pleasant afternoon.

The mind ruptures from the mouth of God.
It bursts the darkness out of you. You reave its deaths.

Response to the Minister of the Cabinet of Doctrines

Outside the Gates of the Jewish cemetery,
cumulus congestus.
Bottle glass, cigarillos, sparrows fighting over Cheetos.
Things pile up.

Turn-of-the-last-century stones set cheek by jowl:
Mandel, Lillie, Tillie, Lester.
So many children.

Every day, I read their names from the road.

One stone set by a scrubby pine abuts
the unfilled field.

I follow the rough stone wall to the bridge across the river,
where the run-off from the Sho-Off car wash
is the only thing that makes the water ripple.

In the bluish pool of light, three female mallards.
Glinting, violet speculums.

In the field, a grave in progress.
It has been like this for days.

B'nai Amoona, Children of Faith,
I think I have nothing for you.

I am constantly right here
in short sleeves, on Shabbat, with my headphones, standing on this wall.

Why am I standing on this wall?

To the mound of opened earth, I sing
whatever song comes through— Tori Amos—*We're in the Wrong Band,*
and I mean it, *let's be sincere,* it's important, I'm serious, *I think that it's time.*

I sing against the limestone
you know that I'm drowning.

I sing into the mortar joints the noise of the water.
I sing into the illusion of the woods.

It pours, and I sing myself a raincoat.

The Mylar star balloon keeps deflating
in the black walnuts, the same way

the little-g god of the water
keeps drifting at me,

or the littler bird,
singing from the lamb on the littlest stone.

Something in its orange breast explodes.

From the Curator of the Interior

Everything important can be said in gelatin silver—
all matters of urgency become solid in acid.
To the ground glass of your eye   these images adhere
and the diffident gaze becomes   electric
immune from static   attuned.

Follow along with your audio guide.
If you do not understand what you are seeing, an attendant will be
happy to adjust your gaze.

Let's proceed into galleries:

"THE MAINBOCHER CORSET"
Horst P. Horst, 1939

The male gaze anticipating the female gaze anticipating the male gaze:
endless corset lacing draping marble:
a woman on a ledge.

"NIGHT-BLOOMING CEREUS"
Sally Mann, 1988

The girl emerging   from the south Virginia woods
The girl wild, emerging
The girl with unopened cactus blooms for breasts
The girl emerging, wild   unopened

"PORTRAIT OF A REPUTATION"
Francesca Woodman, Artist's Book, 1970s

You cannot have copies without an original.
Your hand on your heart   leaves
prints   the most terrible   marks

"BEIJING SCIENCE FICTION"
Friend of the Curator

Christina picks up her long stockings
and begins running

How fleet she is   how swift
Her mouth is full of *Dostoevsky*

In her hair   the elements collapse
        in the smog that hangs over Beijing
        in the car where her body becomes a stoplight
        where the traffic in her eyes is a red debriefment
Wait—
pause her in this heavy moon

        holograph of China, 2012

"Untitled"
Francesca Woodman, MacDowell Colony, 1980

So convincing with your paperbark sleeves
your arms outstretched   your faux bois dress.

"Yet another day alone   I wake up in these white chairs."
When you became the wallpaper, the woods, I did believe you—
Will we always only be waiting for you
to no longer be dead?

"Inadvertent Double Exposure of a Self-Portrait & Images
from Times Square, NYC, 1957"
Diane Arbus

You are your own twin.
You are a twin with Times Square   a twin with despair
You are
        "The Cylcone roller coaster at night, Coney Island,"
        the "Castle at Disneyland" and
        "Rocks on wheels"
"The transvestite at her Birthday Party," you are The Eccentrics,
indelible stain, and one of *them,*
You are *something that was there*
that no longer is.

The Minister of the Cabinet of Self-Preservation

is two-headed—
the desire that impels you
and the fear that unforces your hand.

Be careful on the stairs   because
What if you fell   but kind of
I want to see you fall.

What else shall I imagine if not the worst?

In a dream, the dorsal fin we swim with
is curved, benign
but it may very well be
so it might as well be
a shark's.

And if it swims into the shallows, do I insist upon
what I know to be the opposite and pull myself and my mother out?
How she protests   *Oh, Stephanie. Don't be ridiculous.*

Is it ridiculous to imagine tumbling down stairs to death?
Do I imagine myself instead as an acrobat   combating death with
   skilled tumblings?

I don't like adrenaline
I don't like weightlessness
I don't like the shrugging off of calculated risk.
But then, I do, I lie,
I take my chances.

I like how the body prepares itself for death.

If I think   *I might slice my hand off with this knife*
it's not because I'm drawn to blood,
but I like to see a cylinder pooling with it
from a hollow needle in my arm.

It's just that things happen every day.

Is it ridiculous to dream of landing upright after all?

But what to make of the clear bull head under water?
What to make of the shark   emerging   on four legs?
Dog of the sea   dog with the dorsal-finned back—
It's coming right at us   I say   *It is coming **for** us.*

PSA from the Broadcast Service of the Interior

Lake Michigan is going to kill you   It is only a matter of time—   a
certain equilibrial mass   that might amount to a Saturday morning
or the number of tokens you can pump into Centipede before you're
forced to admit what you really are—   trapped on the x-axis   in
the vector of a real animal   The dream presents you with many
directions   but you never pick this one   not ever   Arcade-death
was never a serious option   *God doesn't think that way, and neither should
you, Stephanie*   Lake Michigan is beneath you   below the houses
below the cliffs   the impossible cliffs   churning an impossible
Pacific salt-blue   *But there are no cliffs over Lake Michigan*   it dawns
on you   Or it weighs on you   like a gigantic sun   There are no
cliffs but the ones steepening as you're standing on them   There is
nothing pacifying about anything that menaces you in broad daylight
You remind yourself   *You are the gun*   *You are the fixed shooter*   But no
matter which direction you turn   you can't see very well   Maybe
it's the light   Maybe it's something more solid in your eyes   Truly,
even the sunshine has it in for you   You don't see the wave coming
at you from out of the sand   only some cabana boys   rearranging
the earth   so that   *there*   where you came from is now under
water   or impossible to climb back to   and one of them who isn't
moving anything   lies straight to your face   *That isn't how you got
here at all*   No matter how many times you survey the elements of
Lake Michigan—   the sunlight   the cool water   the immovable
shore   the scene reiterates itself   A brightness so insistent it is not to
be trusted   You are here to make a decision   and you turn to the
boy straightening up out of the sand   who says   *That is some heavy
shit*   But not even he sees what it is   (what is it?)   that is going
to do you in

The Chamber of Chronicles

From the near end of the universe, reliquiae:

The largest granite outcrop   dust
   (in handfuls)   red, red clay

         From this (your hands) a sapling pine

         then: sap and needles

         then: species plants & hybrids

—a series of approximations,

fragrant things

A story from among the roses, then—

Graham Thomas   Pilgrim   Mr. Lincoln
                        (whose scarlet petals
                        deepen as they fade)

How can such a small handful of lovers require
so much space?

A catalog of lesser elements
produces a tidelessness
that makes the heart go silent
as a crocodile

    The dog skull   the milk teeth   the organ-pipes of mud daubers

On the shallowest skin of snow
the bird's footprint   is very like the bird.

What should be committed to
in pen and ink   in metadata   in clouds
God forbid, in stone?

Disregard
the moss—   the moss rose stems, all thorns

But look here,   look here—   sweet La France

Her mother's rose,
her mother's mother's

—the thorns imply
the animal

Record the moss and the sky goes wild with starlings—

Why should there be
so much   quavering

out of the lampblack dark?

MEMORANDUM *(Sublimation)*

After the snowmelt
not a true anything in sight

Only rank solubles
of mud

Everything
of mud

The air rising from it
ice to steam

Vapor is one kind
of transgression

The molecules I break into
are another

From the Archivist of the Interior
(Make Yourself Great Again)

                             Don't forget your past—   re-
imagine it   re-gratify your loftiest daydreamsicles

and whip yourself   to stiff peaks   Pull yourself back down
into yourself   Retreat—   gaze longingly

inward   Find your meatiest metadata and
metabolize it—   there's no marrow in tomorrow

Re-gravitate toward   a softer set of facts   —embrace
your weightlessness   Reinflate your marshmallowiest desire

and take it snort it   shoot that shit like mainline divinity
All you've ever done is   all you'll ever have

been able to do   Fix on that, Sugar
What—   you really thought you could change?

From the Outbox of the Minister of the Cabinet of Desire

I fantasize about you
I fantasize I have no feeling for you

At the Assembly of the Governing Bodies *(Red Tape)*

Beside your longing,

    someone takes the minutes
    in a peculiar shorthand

       :oughts & shouldn'ts & wouldn't wes.

A leader   then   a congregation
  —everyone familiar with the verse.

           They ask,

                 What purpose is there in being
                 disagreeable? Unamenable?

<Inquiries about the earnestness of your desire>
Someone produces a mirror, proper shoes

               Temper, temper, little drums

        Time to go out walking

              See—she has unoccupied herself
              Now she is   *persuadable*

Their word

They say,

> *What to do when we are full of lead?*
> *When a waxiness has formed the*
> *medium of our hands?*
>
> *She must join in! Participate!*

Your conscience is nothing but a little red tape.

Enter: the forest of the mind
where, lo, you are heavy and bereft.

> *She has become*
> *an obstacle*
> **an irritant**
> *a salt*
>
> *And she desires*
> *nothing*

And I desire nothing

> *She thinks that there is*
> *nothing*

But what if there is nothing

> *So what if there is nothing*

But what if there is nothing but
this accumulation of aches?

> *Say we sent out rabbits—dozens into*
> *field and forest—*
> *and a low fox running—as if through*
> *fire*

> *Which does she try first to retrieve?*

> *Does she take the hunter with the gun?*

Do I use myself against?

> *Play for her the plaintive cry*
> *The great horned owl's six-throated call*

> *Does she want to see the danger overtake?*

In the vulnerability of daybreak
your hands are full of rabbits

> *Her mouth is full of salt*

> *Do not wait for the field to form a clearing.*
> *Show us an animal in the absence.*

Show me an animal that is without its violence.

From the Minister of the Cabinet of Persuasions

Under the shadow
of a Mississippi Kite,
you are periodically inclined

by the dim circling
in the littleleaf linden.

Its leaves are hearts.

Its flowers can be used to treat palpitations,
a nervous stomach, hysteria.

The shadow is so much larger than the bird
that it ignobles you,
and you are a dimness in its wake.

You are the source
that rakes its prey,
the opacity of
a wandering breach
of sunlight in the leaves.

The air is full of honey.
You argue with yourself, in circles.

In a dream:
Natalie, her mouth
full of bees.

You call to hear her voice say
Hi, this is Natalie—

In this narrow
back-and-forth,
are you hopeful or negligible?

From the Cabinet of Unconsciousness *(Teeth)*

It is recommended that you see someone
for nightmares

Tidal waves   chimera   promontory monsters   keep you
from sleeping   and nothing helps

The irate boar who's chasing you   turns out to only be
a llama   but it's still fanged

What flesh would you not sink into
were you so tusked?

Jungian analysis teaches you
to let the creatures overtake you

—the nightmare is nothing
only a horse in the dark

But in the dream
your analyst overtakes you in the doorjamb

and she is more terrifying
than the loose animal

which does not set out to harm you
but cannot help itself

The Minister of the Cabinet of Indulgences Pardons
the Minister of the Cabinet of Desire

For errant wants   assurances of passing
files lost   data (serendipitously)   not recorded

For the will to will unhappy accidents   averted gazes
the benefits of doubt

For jagged spite and sullied joys   festoons
of blooms   nosegays of swooning disbelief

For every bloodied knife   a blade wiped clean

For every dumpster of hard evidence   a fire in the woods

For every body   a disappeared body   6-mil black plastic   a guy
who knows a guy

For every lie   a judge with milky irises   a hand in his robe   a
hand moving someone else's hand   a wad of yellowed dollars

For every longing hanging dripping in the air   more air around it
a bucket of disinfectant   a discreet team of professionals to scrub you
clean as sunshine   head patted   curls coiled behind the ears
un-undone

No one ever has to know   you think   on and off
more than you ever care to admit

From the Minister of the Cabinet of Equivocations

The wave thought,
The wave mulled,
The wave pondered.

The wave argued with itself over what it had heard:

Either God is a back-formation
of the earth's best elements,
or God is an ergo.

The wave supposed:

The best elements argue eagerly
for God   no God:

      Sand Verbena
      Brain Coral
      Blue Whales
      Abyssopelagic Basket Stars
      Dandelion Siphonophores
      Moon Jellies
      Plume Worms
      Arctic Hydromedusa

But,
ergo, blooming.
ergo, joy.

The wave dithered:

Whatever blooms is either miracle
or aberration,

and despite this eithering
it is joy for now.

Response to the Cabinet of Definitives
(Zoological Fantasy)

After Robert Venturi & Denise Scott Brown's "Ugly and Ordinary
Architecture or The Decorated Shed"

for Lisa Pepper

The Amoco is not
a duck. It is a decorated shed.
Its sign is larger than its building.

Here, are ducks. A mother
and six ducklings, exactly.
I admire each of them
as they waddle in a line
up onto the sandbar in the river.

I cannot imagine six children following me
so obediently.

How they sun themselves.

You *are ducks,* I say aloud
and am pondered by a passerby.

Surely, you are a sign
of something,
with all your sunshine.

The river smells like shit.

On its banks rise
the featherheaded umbels
of Queen Anne's Lace.

NO SWIMMING

NO FISHING

DO NOT PLAY AROUND OR IN THE WATER

says the sign.

CALL TO REPORT A FOUL ODOR

I pause my music
and I dial:

I am calling to report a foul odor

> *…?*

From the River des Peres.

> *…Ma'am??*

The sign says, "Call to report a foul odor,"
and there is one,
so I am.

> *It's a sewer overflow, ma'am….Where are you?*

I am standing under a cloud
shaped like The Big Chicken.

I head south to Prokofiev,
The bird is represented by the flute.

I cross the median to peer down
my old professor's street and wonder—

I cross again to see the eggplant door.

I am cross, seeing Christmas lights in June.
I make the face Augusta will make about this later
in front of her computer.

I take the eggplant door for Kerry, back from Ethiopia,
who just met the boy who will be her son.
I take all the aubergine.

Every time I cross the river, I hear
Saint-Saëns' *Aquarium,*
from the *Carnival of the Animals.*
I take the smoke tree and the rabbit,
whose ears are spoons.
Its body, largely, is its head; its head,
a large and wary eye.
I take the *Personages with Long Ears.*

I say to the bear-dog,
*You are **heroic and original**.*
Behind the chain-link, he barks to my whistles.

I take the speckled eggs, the nest,
the *Aviary* from the rose's crotch of limbs.

The claret kerchief
from the flicker's head,
its wings the color of the sun.

I take the girl with the flouncing red curls.

I take the eastern kingbird and the blue jay
piping the *Barber of Seville*
through the exhaust of a city bus.

Plied with symbols, I bend to take
a bird's black feather—no, the bird's *shoulder*,
tipped red with flesh and bright with bone.

Riposte to the Cabinet of Consolations

Here's what we know

about Harvey   In a 1,000-year flood   we are glazed over
with disconsolate florals   unnatural violets   hyperpale

lilac   The only new ideas we introduce
are new colors for the maps

The people of Houston are empurpled
by rain   Harvey is self-

fulfilling   self-inundating   It sucks up its own
water   and spits it back out   while people

point to people   as silver linings   as if
a baby's drowned mother could float   like

a cloud   The human effect system is buoyed
by ideas   of mother as life raft   one instead of

the other   We falter while we prosper
but blithely   with just the kind of thinking that sinks us

MEMORANDUM *(Ubiquity)*

In the foreground of winter
an amethyst   of ice

From this season of white outcroppings
a profusion of violets

You weren't how you imagined yourself

Your eyes were full of   allium
Your mouth mouthed,

    O, immortal information
    O, forgetting

You were nostalgic for times that weren't how you imagined they
would be

Your mouth was full of wild onions
You said

    The bulb of the blossom
    is the bulb of the root

And your eyes went wild
and your mind went wild completely

Your mouth went purple around the wildness
You imagined everything   but differently

    O, ubiquity
    What do I do with your everything, everywhere?

The Minister of the Cabinet of Bespoke Futures

always countered with a revival model
—a neo-neo-Gothic version
of the facts.

For your empire of failure   she offers
limestone colonnades   oak allées   granite fortifications
to buttress all your monocultural desires.

It was an academic exercise—   wanting
to be weightless   hoping
for something more.

When the sky opens up
your desktop says something
in auspicious botspeak:

            THE CLOUDS ARE CLEARING, STEPHANIE

Promises, promises.
I wasn't trying to be sanguine—
I was only staring indirectly at the sun.

            WEATHER WOULD LIKE TO OPEN "THE WEATHER"

I would like to open myself, too.
I would like to feel something new
over   and   over   and   over   again.

Say something evidenceless
Say something moody-broody

            STORMS ARE HEADED YOUR WAY, STEPH

How can you tragedize so breezily?
You can't burn your eyes out on a glass star.
Say something beyond atmosphere.

> Okay.
> *Find*: The Path of Totality

Find me some other quartz-y spiral
where I can mineralize uninterrupted.

> Okay.
> *Find*: Life on other planets

No, don't say: Imagine the difference between you and them
Say: Imagine every open mouth as a possibility for more than
        conversation
Say: What are you waiting for

> Okay.
> *Find*: Porn

Overhead, the news broadcasts off the blade of a fan.
The Nation's id is talking again—

(on and off) and (on and off)

—*Just tell me the lie I want to believe in*
Say: I can make you louder than them.

> Please check all the boxes you are interested in
> Please check all the boxes you are interested in
> Please check all the boxes you are interested in

From the Minister of the Cabinet of Admonition

God gave you fire
but told you to be careful
when you used it

You could use it whenever you wanted
but you could never be
careful enough

You resented God every time
a flame coiled out of your mouth
with a mouth of its own

God is always playing tricks
you said   or the fire said
You were never sure which

From the Cabinet of Unconsciousness
(Well Waiting Room)

You go to the room on the right   You go to the mute blue cube   that is distinctly unevocative   that nothing can divide   The magazines the puzzles   cannot interest you a minute   They cannot distract you from the glass view of other children   Some of them don't seem sick either but they are   Be glad for the clarity because let's not talk about things as if they're vellum when everything is inked clear You know something's wrong with you   You have been on both sides of this barrier   You have been small and dangerously fevered   You have been the child vomiting down her mother's back You have been cooled by a stainless basin and sent home undistressed You have been examined while being examined   Indeed   you have been scrutinized   But you have been frank   You have been snide   You have been dishonest about your body when your body has been lobbed against you   The details of your body have been catalogued   You have been weighed and calipered   You are larger than the other children, now   *You are hardly a child, anymore*   You are large and off the charts   and your doctor frightens you   about incremental weight gain   and pubic lice   and toxic shock   and scarring   and tearing   and contagion   and masturbating   as if *that's* a cure   as if that's the only other option   And no one ever says anything   No one ever talks about need   or the spikes to your system   or about sadness   or about sadness   No one has tried anything uncompartmentalized   No one has tried to do anything but contain it   *You know   I can't help it*   You tell her that   No one has done anything out of the ordinary

At the Assembly of the Governing Bodies, the Minister of the Cabinet of Oversight Makes a Motion to Consolidate, and the Speaker of the House of the Interior Just Goes Along with It

—not even the Minister of the Cabinet of Despair was permitted

to make a motion   though she was so moved

so often   Though she struggled to contain

her composure   Though her members pleaded for decency

over sport   Though she presented fine evidence

Though she was genuine   and spoke plainly

and only for herself   But when she was told

when to speak   and to whom   and at what length   and at whose pleasure

something overcame her   When forced

she spoke for everyone   on the floor

and she took everyone

down with her

The Minister of the Cabinet of Immateriality

decided what should stay and what should have been
trashed long ago   *No more*

bullshit   she would say
on a tear   dumping things

over the side   bewildering
the midshipmen—   who were not even men

at all   but some persons
of some substance   some solid

stock   (the stuff that legend's
stuffed with)   —who watched things

going overboard   left and right
Aye, aye!   the bright things plunging

light and delicate   into the surf
And periodically and at intervals

a body going after them
oftentimes   at her own peril

The body following   hoping
for salvation   an act of consequence

and (maybe) valor   The body going after that
after *maybe*   *maybe if*

going after the singingfish   the body lost
in singing   but no matter

because   the thing of it
is   the thing of it   is gone

MEMORANDUM *(Withholdings)*

The cloud was not withholding
You withhold nothing   you give up your storms

The cloud was withholding
its fullness was unnerving   and it swelled to armor
And you   with your gray molecules—
even your heart has a false back

From the Cabinet of Unconsciousness *(Whaling)*

There is a whale

Your mother sees it

She calls to you

    There is a whale!

And her exuberance

is the exuberance of its tail   surfacing

As a sharp blade draws blood

this draws blood back to the body

Back to all the parts that had been dying

There is a whale!

You say to the person standing next to you

But she does not see it

It is terrible that no one else sees it

From the Minister of the Cabinet of Ordinary Affairs

The governing bodies   disagree:

One busies herself   responding   The other

talks about sharp objects

The self   divided thusly   notes:

every day   dogs re-bark their grievances

The cabinet becomes   a place for filling emptinesses

—You must eat <u>something</u>

all morning   with a mouse on your tongue

Something becomes   dimensional   belated

a body in a wake

It sprouts in you
a cypress
with high branches   dropping needles

—your fist on the glass

raw as a mineral

Out at the raincloud:

                    A dark bird   on wet bark

          in its beak   the flesh of another animal

   —your open palm

is full
of glass

Your stomach winces   tight as a cabbage

The Cabinet of Lesser Offenses

cannot help itself   It endeavors
toward disaster

An orchestra of secondary pleasures
it speaks in horns and trumpets
in capitals   imperatives   swears indecently

Senses what is pliable and leaps
                precipitando   *(falling)*

toward laziness   impetuousness   schadenfreude

Skirts the edges   bassoon and string
to pacify
                andante
the anxiety that is its waste

Crimes against others are crimes against the self
                -issimo, -etto   *(more or less)*

What *of* your vices?   it prepares them
           placido
on a plate

Is it a weakness or window, it asks *capriccioso*   *(fancifully)*

and sends its dog for   fetching *Arco!*
           Arco—pronto!

                    (with the bow)

He offers himself obediently
slides on his paws   through leaves and straw
fetches back   a human heart   holds it

                            pesante
                                         (heavily)

in his maw   and does not break
the membrane of its chambers

If offered a hand   he will eat out of it
                            a piacere   *(at pleasure)*
or he will lick it   clean to bone

From the Minister of the Cabinet of Retribution

The god who served as messenger to the gods
was the god of thieves   and commerce
Most transactions are a kind of reputable theft

and transferring messages   between the living and the dead
weight of our lives   isn't always fair trade
What language is ever legal tender?

The merchandise of our former selves   is something
to be bargained for   Settle on a figure for what you'd pay
to have it all backor never see any of it

again   The god of boundaries can get
right up in your business—   everything you say has value
and some words cost you   more than others

Tell me   is a kind of begging
between lovers   a positioning of one body
under another   *Tell me this means nothing*

is a promise you're made to make   lying
across a hotel bed   And if you could ask
whatever god you wanted   or if you could just get a god

to pick up the phone   —even if you have to pay
by the minute   or maybe if the messenger
god of the gods could take a fucking memo   from the living

to the living   for once   you might say
Whatever in my life I've taken   —write this down—
I did not deserve this

From the Analyst of the Anterior

Now that you have found your way out   let's think about the next
time   you find yourself   unimaginably   irrevocably   inexorably
trapped   Let's say you are on a boat   No—don't *pretend* you are on
a boat   *Say*   **I am on a boat**   What does your insistence permit
you   What idolatries   What tender exchanges   You are on a boat
disallowing nothing   lolling   back and forth   and   back and
forth   and   (that's it)   back and forth   against the waves   And
maybe there's   a dalliance   or   a meandering   or   a complete
breach of faith   What's the worst that can happen   when you are
on a boat   (keep saying it)   You aren't trapped anywhere really   are
you   So might you not   just drift out   after all   unafraid

MEMORANDUM *(Impasse)*

No outlet at the intake   —an impasse
the river crosses *you*

Your vulnerable, unchambered self stands
shin-deep in ice floe

:things precipitate

Light breaks from the mackerel
and settles on the craquelure of old boots

A dusky bird breaches the bark
and scatters the orangest hours across the snow

Altocumulus:

the hour raises a cloud-high thought

    :

I am the animal at the foothill
I am sooted   and motifed

The high cloud   exits
and I go gray with foxtails

It exits
yes   it exits me

From the Cabinet of Unconsciousness *(No Man's Land)*

after Lisa Yuskavage

for Jessica Baran

I had a nightmare, Jessica   I had another nightmare   I had
another one and you're the only one I can tell   I tell you not in so
many words   not in these exact words   I tell you nothing exactly
I tell you this but not that   I say I was two things   split in the acid
I say I was two people   split in the light   I was unhappy   I was
married   I was unhappily married   to a woman like a painting   like
a Yuskavage painting   but savagely boned   I tell you I was doubling
in the amniotic green light   and should I tell you   can I tell you
the real nightmare terrifying me from the inside   The real nightmare
was I didn't know her at all   But I knew her, yeah?   I knew her like
a painting   a Yuskavage painting   and there were her bones   all laid
out   unnerving   I knew her like two people   like how two people
know   how to terrify each other   from the inside out   I convinced
myself *I know her*   I looked at her like *I know her*   like I knew those
terrifying eyes   like I was this but not that   And just like that   I
told you   I terrified her from the inside out   Just like that painting
that Yuskavage painting   in a plume of green light   And you said
Yeah, there's something to that   I don't what to do with that

The Minister of the Cabinet of Decorum

after Louise Bourgeois

always hated Louise
because Louise was always substituting
one thing for another

        Abstracting rage as desire   orgasm as metonym
        but no one's ever getting off
        Louise insisted her clouds weren't dicks

but then what was she planning
on using that knife for?
Louise saw things through a man's eyes

        so when she cut out his eyes
        she saw nothing at all
        Louise made the Minister see

her own body as
a hideous double negative
in degrading rubber   while Louise

        —why Louise remained pristine
        as marble   but as full of holes
        and phallocentric as Pietrasanta plasters

The Minister thought Louise was a dick
because Louise was self-
cannibalizing   Louise prepared

                    a dinner for the family
                    of the family
                    and then she ate the family

The Minister was never allowed
to do anything of the sort
at the dinner table

                    or anyplace else   for that matter
                    The Minister resented the implication
                    that *this* was that   or that *she* was that

She resented the confrontation
and she resented she
had to be the Minister at all

                    But she held her tongue
                    as she was taught to do
                    like an unswallowable

piece of gristle
You bite your tongue—
she'd say to herself

> *You pretend that it's delicious*
> *—and don't you ever let anyone*
> *see you spit it out*

The Minister of the Cabinet of Covenants Argues with the Minister of the Cabinet of Desire

He wasn't hers.
He wasn't *hers* either.

The Cabinet of Reason

gives answers to God
Hardhearted echolalias   we bay like dogs.

When God asks,
why are you crying out to me?
we pillar ourselves:
in cloud   or salt   or fire

God asks so many questions

We think ourselves   though fitful   full of purpose
Purposefully   we think ourselves a dog
    with   *eyes the size of saucers*
    or   *eyes the size of millstones*
    or   *eyes like the round tower*

and the dogs light out
unquestioning

But when God shouts
we extend our hands

We think ourselves a wall of water
   we retrieve
   we carry
we walk right through

The Minister of the Cabinet of Confrontations

after Anne Carson

approximates the facts   approaches them cautiously
as facsimile   as something else

Some measure of protection—   she opens her mouth
and blows glass all around her   or

a spray of thorns or
armor or
trumpeting or
tar or
honey or
smoke or
vapors or
poisonous vapors

A ground glass green
with ropes all around it

and the air becomes   italicized   a tonic   tolerable

so we understand each other
as other
as people do

The Minister of the Cabinet of Vengeance
Issues a Decree

after Shakespeare's Sonnet 135

Whether you knew it or not   there are holes
in everything   Drill down to where

you think you'll find   intention   or   your sense
of moral fortitude   or   resolution   or   absolute

jurisdiction   Every opening is an opportunity
to fill a space with questions about what falls

within the boundaries of authority   Porosity is the mouth of
trumpery gaping at you to muck it up   Fill each gap

with a paste of CMYK unmistakability   Smooth
the finish   Make all your holes as proud

and fertile as a crowd gathering   preparing
to revolt   Bore your own hole through the most illegitimate

idea of leadership   Make all your voids
both vast and overflowing   —too much

for even the thickest rope to wick
True your marks   De-escalate something   De-

masculate something   Gnaw your way through
Solicit your friends   your sisters   your comrades

your compatriots—   Divine
all your deepest wonders   and join in!

Take joy in putting things asunder!   Revel in what
you can unravel with *your broad and spacious will*

To the Cabinet of Ambivalences *(UNANSWD/UNHRD)*

Going to and from somewhere,
I pass a group of happy children
shouting *Lemonade!*

and when I do not stop
they instead shout *Loser!*
and I know they're right.

But they're not selling what I want, and who is?
It does not seem producible.

It is not this house on the corner,
which is the size of a dormitory
and equal in its charm.

I do not covet this, Reince Priebus.
I have no romance for the tiny assholes running the lemonade stand.

That is *someone's* dream, American and unexceptional.

In my palm, a digital map locates me in a roundabout as
a pulsing, blue dot.
I cannot get anywhere from here.

Why do I not want lemonade?
Why do I not participate?

I watch people on television, traveling.

I listen to Neil Armstrong radioing from the moon.

Over and over, I scan the transcripts of
Earhart circling Howland Island:

WE ARE UNABLE TO HEAR YOU
TO TAKE A BEARING

PLS TAKE BEARING ON US
AND ANS [US] WID VOICE

What can I make
with intermittent despair?

An engine roars, and I look up
to see the sun caught in the fuselage
of a jet. I wave.

DO YOU HEAR MY SIGNALS

WILL U PLS ACKNOWLEDGE

And then all my thoughts are icy blue
with frigate birds and parachutes
and I am filled with cumulus and cannot see.

KHAQQ CLNG ITASCA

WE MUST BE ON YOU
BUT CANNOT SEE U

Knowing I begin and end with images,
how far across this field
can my voice extend in singing, in screaming?

From the Press Secretary of the Interior
(Confirmed Reports)

We have confirmed reports
the ▮▮▮▮▮▮▮ exists.

We have differing reports.

We have varying accounts of
the sighting of the ▮▮▮▮▮▮

But we can confirm for you today
that ▮▮▮▮▮ exists,
that it is—extraordinary;
but not the only one.

For two appeared this morning—
<gasping>
a pair of females—
and their bodies were unequaled.
Like dogs the size of horses.
Like emus with the heads of dogs.
And some have said
like wolves
and some have said
with horns
and some have seen
a double tusk of onyx
which the animal bares
when it becomes
determined, all jaw,
your number in its mouth.

***

Divine strangeness by intimacy
What is strange has been polluted by   what is ordinary
     familiar

Is it muddled? Muddied? Watered down?
What frightens you about something *so* innocuous?

The innocuousness.

Everyone is becoming their own era. Post- world.

               ***

You have asked about the proposed restrictions
on the ▮▮▮▮▮▮ —and I have stated
and I will tell you
—I have said that those proposals came from
outside this administration—
The Minister will not approve that—
She will not affiliate
or be a party to—
any program that encroaches upon the ▮▮▮▮▮▮
—that waters down or separates into
solutions and precipitants—   And furthermore—
And furthermore—
In the ▮▮▮▮▮▮ you have shown her—
And you have made it very clear—
I can confirm that she has seen the ▮▮▮▮▮▮
—and she is willing
She is willing to defend the ▮▮▮▮▮▮
—she understands the consequences—

She acknowledges and will protect the ▮▮▮▮▮▮▮ —I tell you
I tell you—
I tell you she is willing.

***

THE RAINCLOUD HOVERED.

It hovered over the body.

The rain hovered over
and shouldered its weight.

Before the body,
an arrangement of injurious roses.

The water hovered ponderously
and shielded the body from its own weight.

***

It is not unusual to have dreams about waves. Your mother, your sister. Not unusual. Not nightmares. Nightmares. Either/or. The bottlenose shark. The sheepshead shark. Heads, high as a bookcase. Sharks that tunnel boxy along canals. Beyond the animal, and what is animal. Whatever bears a planetary tooth. And you must weigh how much you wish to be in the water against the danger of being swallowed whole. Dreams of waves are common. Common, dreams of the sea. Dreams of tides and tidalness. All waves coming at once. The colossal single wave that balances you barely. The small you, atop the wine-dark sea.

MEMORANDUM *(Overstory)*

The Earth knew God was disappointed

The Earth knew it
it knew it
it knew it

The Earth saw
what God had intended—

the peach tree
ridiculously overblossomed

The Earth had so many things
—a wilderness of orchards

From the Cabinet of Survival Mechanisms

When the tests come back   I make
deepfakes of both of us   In this life   my mother does not have
a rectangular gray screen behind her irises   or   that is the worst
of our problems   I make like I'm good at writing fantasy   and she's good at
living it   We see nothing of concern   When the doctor asks
Where does it hurt   my mother says   *It's like a shoulder holster—I watch a lot of*
crime procedurals   but then someone—maybe it's Jim Henson—hands her
a six-shooter   and now *we* run the joint   I don't mind being felt
on a green screen   I don't mind being tethered to my actor
through a small, steel rod   I don't mind the stitching
hitching us together   Our lungs are massive now   We are
almost at capacity   We talk about the news   about politics
FakeMe says   *If that man were the root of the problem   I'd kill him myself*
I would too   FakeMom says   *I've thought about it   I wish we could*
do it together   and get away with it   (My mother would be
so good at that   really   she's a realist)   *Watch me*   she says
like she would never ever say   *I think I make a pretty hot cowgirl*

From the Cabinet of Unconsciousness *(Unremittingness)*

The waves came in and out for days without breaking
      anything

As if the sea were only   a bay

As if we were only   lagooned

But the sea was no matter anyhow

Because the sea was [at]
      the sea was [there]
      the sea was [where we]
      the sea was [only getting around it]

And so
     no breaking

no backdrop
no territory
no intrusion

But a foreground, yes

     buildings
     lit up from the inside

     people trapped in houses

A foreground, yes
A foreground of fire

From the Minister of the Cabinet of Reason
(re: Your Indulgent Hopefulness in an Afterlife)

Since you have decided you cannot live without God,
everything is externalized as damages—you bruise like fruit.

You wear your spleen
like chain mail
or a choke chain
or a locket of blood—
as if you could forget what blood tastes like.

The dead are always on the tip of your tongue,
the dead are underfoot.
Animals disappear, and you are one of them.

Is everything a portent?
Is anything not messaging?
The tiniest remains leave you gasping.

The white skin of the carcass.
The small bones of the carcass.
The hairlessness.
The scentlessness.
The smoothness of the carcass.
A pencil-mark mouth.
An un-emerged eye.
A chalky firstling.

You find it before the blowflies or the fire ants
as if nothing had ever touched it—
in unmitigated, solid oblivion.

But you see everything as full and tender.
The flesh produces
and it blooms like a god.

But put your skin on its skin
your pale on its pale—
You are supple. You stick.
In your rawest valve
can't you feel the definitiveness of your exile?
This is no important reckoning.

There is no sweetness
in this ceaseless tripping over death.

The Minister of the Cabinet of Disasters

couldn't stop herself from seeing it
couldn't not look   couldn't bury it

She was in it up to her stocking heels   her bootpulls   her brass
buttons   her cotton casuals   her epaulettes   She was in it
up to her sockets

and her most delicate nerve endings bristled
in the dust

Other ministers retreated
to their districts—   took shelter

beneath heavy objects   prayed
in doorjambs   held hands   pissed themselves

But the Minister steadied herself
against the rubble   burned a headlamp through
the smokeblack corridors

She tweezed the shrapnel from your palms
gauzed your wounds   unburred your shredded edges   and
carried you to water   She held you

though the buildings scorched around you
as though there was never anything but burning

From the Minister of the Cabinet of Unconsciousness
(Natalie & the Waves)

Take Natalie with you when you go to see the waves.

There is a viewing box and the crowds will gather.

The crowds that gather there will be great.

Take Natalie, for the waves are great.

Take Natalie with you if you have to see the waves.

Take Natalie, because everything you've heard is true.

The waves are as tall as they are wide.

How thin they are.

How fragile.

How vulgarly they tremble.

How terrifyingly.

How they buckle instead of break.

Take Natalie with you because you love her for fathoms.

Take Natalie. You don't want to go alone.

The waves come in like a rolling horizon.

The waves pile up like buildings, one on the other.

The waves become like architecture, and Natalie is an architect, bring her.

The waves have mass and axes and equilibrium.

The waves are rolling, load-bearing walls.

Take Natalie with you and the weight of it will be nothing.

Take Natalie, take an architect of the sea.

Take her because the water can be only somewhat honest with you.

Take Natalie.

The water's iodine.

The water's glass.

The water's the dusk of the earth.

Take Natalie with you.

Tie your hands together.

Braid your hair together.

Make a pact together before the sea.

Hold together as the water overtakes you.

The water brines the top of your throat.

Hold together as you become salt.

MEMORANDUM *(Verisimilitude)*

The Venn diagram of Life and Death contained   a lot
     of misinformation   The middle was where we did

most of our living worth living for   bumping up against
     Death's membrane   Death's skin   only

an arm's length away   a breath's   Press your lips against Death's
     round belly   This is what everyone calls gravity

Bulletins from the Cloud Cabinet

for Jana Harper

The raincloud hovered distantly.
The raincloud sensed the approach.
The raincloud wanted for nothing and gave of itself freely.
The raincloud drifted wantonly.
The raincloud took to hairpin tunnels.
The raincloud knew vastness.
The raincloud was massive, but ignored its physicality.
The raincloud became a membrane and stretched itself to volume.
The raincloud was all mass.
The raincloud steadied itself against the darkness.
The raincloud felt distant in its new volume.
The raincloud swelled and surrounded itself with pangs of light.
The raincloud surrounded itself with what it could not avoid.
The raincloud had its habits, and clung to its rituals.
The raincloud clung to rituals and they sustained it.
The raincloud shifted with a sudden weight.
The raincloud held on and its habits were a comfort.
The raincloud held fast through what moved through it.
The raincloud shifted and shifted in the suddenness.
The raincloud held, though the pangs could not, though the darkness could not.
The raincloud clung.

Rebuttal from the General Counsel of the Interior

Imagine God as a woman   No paternal longing for   no
husbanding   no heroism—well, yes, heroism   but no hero
complex   no heroics   No masculinizing of feminizing   No god
as a goddess   No god with a dick   Imagine God as something else
entirely   But, robes, yes   Knowing, yes   Loving, yes   For
God's sake make your god a loving god   Broad-shouldered and
thick   Or rangy   long-legged   long in the tooth   Longed for
and longing for   forsaken   forlorn   taken for granted   taken
for a fool   Take your worst image of God   —imagine your god as
that   Make your god inferior in some other god's eyes   Make that
god love your god anyway   Imagine your god as my god—just—let's
say that it's true   Let's say   all we have is each other   Imagine
how yours   (as mine)   loves me   (as you)

From the Press Secretary of the Interior
(Gravitational Waves)

They proved this week we're all in this together.
Every time we move we disrupt something

intimately. Time is flexible and your life is woozy gelatin.
Draw a blade across and you might grow

to believe you are self-healing. But you cried out
and someone else absorbed the waves of pain

you sent cascading outward. Someone so
remotely distant from you saw the big one

coming and let it overcome her.
Someone nearer clung to filmy buoys and knew

your sorrow deeply. But the nearest one—
the very nearest to you—took it in

the gut, and you trembled at how she stomached it
and survived. You understood the reach

of love—you walked away with proof
that starry nets will bear your every grief.

From the Minister of the Cabinet of Unconsciousness
(Lesser Animals)

You come to a clearing   A clearing is a place you enter into after
having been lost within something   like a hedge maze   or a thicket
or a forest of thought   but before you've actually found your way
out   A clearing is not a way out   In the clearing   things you
had lived without—   direct sunlight   sky   rainclouds   open air
The thicket is around you   but you photosynthesize automatically
Animals appear   spotlit   like a parade—   an elephant   a Siberian
tiger   hippopotamus   oryx   zebra   —but miniature   like kittens
And the clearing   now   so immensely vast   All of these emerged
from the thicket   All of them   were in there with you

NOTES

Many of the poems in this book were written as ekphrastic responses to the news, primarily live broadcasts of the PBS NewsHour, which I have watched virtually every night since childhood, and am greatly indebted to. Occasionally, I have incorporated fragments of phrases uttered spontaneously by journalists and interview subjects, along with facts and statistics, as found language. The notes below account for the most specific instances of inspiration and quotation not otherwise accounted for on the pages in which the poems appear.

"The Ambassador of the Interior Has a Talking To with the Minister of the Cabinet of Vengeance" was inspired by the phrase "Civilization started small" uttered in the *Civilizations* documentary series on PBS.

"The Cabinet of Slippery Slopes" was written as part of an ekphrastic-by-mail collaboration with the artist Michael J. Byron.

"From the Curator of the Interior" contains quotes from both Francesca Woodman and Diane Arbus; sadly, my notes fail to indicate the books in which I found them.

In "The Cabinet of Reason," "eyes the size of saucers . . . eyes like the round tower," is taken from Hans Christen Andersen's "The Tinder Box," a terrifying and alluring story I listened to (on a record!) as child as I fell asleep.

"From the Cabinet of Unconsciousness *(Teeth)*." A Jungian analyst I saw about my persistent nightmares told me to think of them literally as *night mares*—horses in the dark.

"The Minister of the Cabinet of Bespoke Futures" contains phrases taken from and inspired by notifications from my iPhone, Facebook, laptop computer, and the Internet.

In "To the Cabinet of Ambivalences (UNANSWD/UNHRD)," the lines "I do not covet this, Reince Priebus./I have no romance for the tiny assholes running the lemonade stand" were inspired by a mendacious trope promulgated by Republicans at the 2012 Republican National Convention. At the event, then RNC chair Reince Priebus asserted that "President Obama's private business experience hasn't seen the inside of a lemonade stand." Somehow equating this lapse in boyhood entrepreneurship with anti-Americanism, he pushed further: "This President looks down on American free enterprise.... That makes me think Barack Obama has a problem with the American Dream." Sources: *The New Yorker* and Politico.

Acknowledgments

My deep gratitude to the readers and editors of the following journals and outlets, where these poems first appeared: *AGNI, Another Chicago Magazine, Bennington Review, Best New Poets 2015, Black Warrior Review, Bomb, Burnside Review, Cincinnati Review, Columbia: A Journal of Literature and Art, Denver Quarterly, Diagram, Fence, The Florida Review, Georgia Review, Harp & Altar, Harvard Review, Iowa Review, LIT, NECK Press, OmniVerse, PoetryNow,* the Poetry Foundation website, *Poetry Northwest, Seneca Review, Smartish Pace, South Dakota Review, Sou'wester, Sprung Formal, Tarpaulin Sky, Tupelo Quarterly, Washington Square Review,* and *Yew*.

Enormous thanks to my family and friends for your encouragement and your inspiration.

To American public media outlets, thank you for setting and keeping the record straight.

To Cheryl Wassenaar—collaborating with you is a gift.

To Arny, who lives with all of the voices in this book—you hold me together. You have all my love.

And, to my mother—always and forever.

Stephanie Ellis Schlaifer is a poet and installation artist in St. Louis. She is the author of the poetry collection *Cleavemark* (BOAAT Press, 2016) and the children's book *The Cloud Lasso* (Penny Candy Books, 2019). Her poems and art have appeared in *Bomb, Bennington Review, Georgia Review, Harvard Review, Iowa Review, AGNI, Washington Square, At Length, The Offing, Denver Quarterly, LIT, Colorado Review,* and on PoetryNow and the Poetry Foundation website, among others. She frequently collaborates with other artists, most recently with Cheryl Wassenaar on the installation *The Cabinet of Ordinary Affairs* at the Des Lee Gallery. Her work can be viewed at stephanieschlaifer.com.

Nancy K. Pearson

The Whole by Contemplation of a Single Bone

Daneen Wardrop

Cyclorama

Terrence Chiusano

On Generation & Corruption

Sara Michas-Martin

Gray Matter

Peter Streckfus

Errings

Amy Sara Carroll

Fannie + Freddie: The Sentimentality of Post–9/11 Pornography

Nicolas Hundley

The Revolver in the Hive

Julie Choffel

The Hello Delay

Michelle Naka Pierce

Continuous Frieze Bordering Red

Leslie C. Chang

Things That No Longer Delight Me

Amy Catanzano

Multiversal

Darcie Dennigan

Corinna A-Maying the Apocalypse

Karin Gottshall

Crocus

Jean Gallagher

This Minute

Lee Robinson

Hearsay

Janet Kaplan

The Glazier's Country

Robert Thomas

Door to Door

Julie Sheehan

Thaw

Jennifer Clarvoe

Invisible Tender

Lightning Source UK Ltd.
Milton Keynes UK
UKHW010745110921
389953UK00012B/467

9 780823 297771